Kel's Bad Leg

By Debbie Croft

T0360169

Kel and Jed went on a run.

"I run a lot," said Kel.

"I can win!"

"I run a lot, too," said Jed.
"I can win!"

Kel and Jed ran and ran.

Kel hit his leg on
a big wet log.

"Look, Jed! My leg!" said Kel.

"Sit on the log, Kel!"
said Jed.
"I can run and get Mum."

Mum and Jed got Kel
in the van.

"My leg is bad!" said Kel.

Kel was sad.

"I did not win, Jed!" said Kel.

CHECKING FOR MEANING

1. What did Kel hit his leg on? *(Literal)*

2. How did Kel get to the hospital? *(Literal)*

3. What do you think the weather was like when Kel and Jed were running? How do you know? *(Inferential)*

EXTENDING VOCABULARY

and	Look at the word *and*. Which letters can be added to the front of *and* to make a new word?
said	Look at the word *said*. What is the tricky part of this word? What words do you know that mean the same as *said*?
wet	The log that Kel falls on is *big* and *wet*. What other words could be used to describe the log?

MOVING BEYOND THE TEXT

1. What do you think happened after the story ended?

2. Do you like running? Why or why not?

3. What are some other things that you like to do with friends and family?

4. Who would you go to for help if you were hurt or had an accident?

SPEED SOUNDS

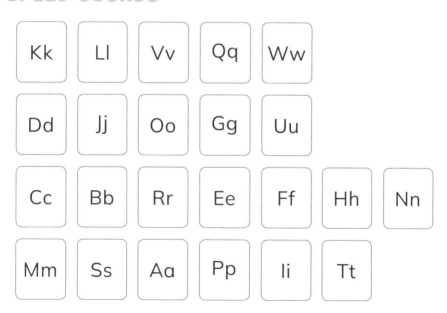

Kk	Ll	Vv	Qq	Ww		
Dd	Jj	Oo	Gg	Uu		
Cc	Bb	Rr	Ee	Ff	Hh	Nn
Mm	Ss	Aa	Pp	Ii	Tt	

PRACTICE WORDS

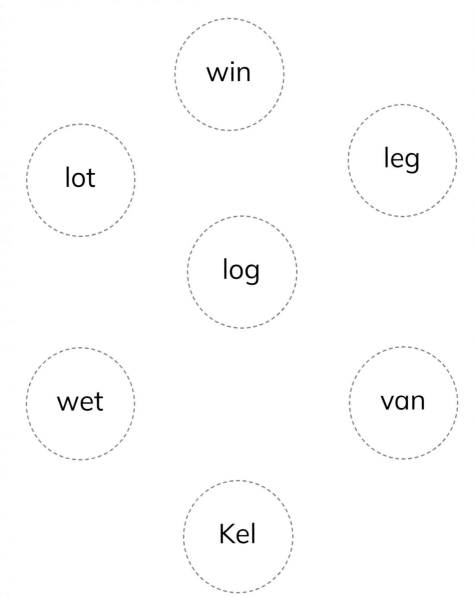

win

lot

leg

log

wet

van

Kel